IMAGES
of America

SCHERERVILLE

IMAGES
of America

SCHERERVILLE

Sandi Radoja

ARCADIA
PUBLISHING

Published by Arcadia Publishing
Charleston, South Carolina

Printed in the United States of America

Library of Congress Control Number: 2022941316

For all general information, please contact Arcadia Publishing:
Telephone 843-853-2070
Fax 843-853-0044
E-mail sales@arcadiapublishing.com
For customer service and orders:
Toll-Free 1-888-313-2665

Visit us on the Internet at www.arcadiapublishing.com

*This book is dedicated to the all-volunteer Schererville Historical
Society for preserving photographs and volumes of town history and
to my ever-patient husband, whose encouragement
and guidance made it possible.*

CONTENTS

In the meantime, the Chicago & Great Eastern Railroad arrived, with the first tracks running right through what is now downtown Schererville. This railroad later became the Pennsylvania Railroad and changed its name again after that to be known as Conrail. Those first tracks crossed at the very point where the Town of Schererville kicked off its centennial celebration in 1966. That was not a coincidence, but a planned homage.

Around the time John Thiel opened his blacksmith shop in 1870, a dairy was opened across the street by Michael Grimmer. A general store was also opened by Grimmer. Like a snowball downhill, more businesses got their start as men recognized the growing need and grabbed at opportunities. A saloon, a cigar factory, an icehouse, a grocery store, a meat market, and more popped up. These enterprises were started by men with now familiar names such as Austgen, Lustig, Schulte, and Schubert.

Research revealed that Jacob Scholl established a carpentry shop in town around this same time. That alone is not a significant fact, but of interest is that Scholl was the father of Dr. William Mathias Scholl, who found fame—and at least some degree of fortune—in foot products. Reportedly, the younger Scholl worked in a shoe store somewhere locally in northwest Indiana. From those humble beginnings, he invented and patented the first arch support for footwear in the early 20th century. Dr. Scholl's has become a household name forever associated with foot care, and now some of us will also associate it with Schererville.

On September 5, 1911, the civil Town of Schererville was incorporated. The men who served on the committee to reach this milestone included Jacob Scholl, John A. Mager, Sarinis P. Swets, Peter A. Grimmer, and Frank Berwanger. When the citizens voted in the first town board, Scholl, Mager, and Swets were elected, while Grimmer was chosen to serve as the first clerk and Berwanger the first treasurer.

Another Grimmer family member was township trustee Michael Grimmer, who witnessed the completion of the first stone road. By 1911, it would be paved. Two years later, the first Lincoln Highway Association was formed, and by 1916, the Federal Road Aid Act was enacted to assist in developing what became US 30. This major highway runs across the entire country from New York to California. US 41, which runs from its northern point in the Upper Peninsula of Michigan, through Schererville, and continues south all the way to Miami, Florida, crosses US 30 in the town of Schererville.

Just as they did in the time Native Americans inhabited this area, today's residents and travelers make daily use of the trails that crisscross Schererville. But these are now the modern trails of a complex and sophisticated national highway system. They are used by thousands every single day, as we have become a society that functions and depends on motorized travel.

From Indian trails to modern highways, Schererville was then, is now, and will likely always be known as the "Crossroads of the Nation."

One

EARLY DAYS

There are at least two dates representing the beginning of the town of Schererville. The official founding took place on April 10, 1866, when one of the original settlers, Nicholas Scherer, recorded the plat. He was a German immigrant who had been in the area for 20 years. Scherer purchased the property soon after his arrival from a gentleman named Aaron Hart. The swampland had been transformed into tillable soil through the construction of ditches designed to manage drainage. Hart Ditch was created to drain into Plum Creek, which carries water to the Little Calumet River. Hart had already made his mark in the neighboring town of Dyer. Scherer called his newly platted town by his family name, while Hart named Dyer using his wife's maiden name.

The industrious Scherer worked for the State of Indiana as a swampland drainer and land commissioner, which certainly gave him somewhat of an advantage in establishing the town. In that capacity, he was administering lands under the Federal Swamp Land Act of 1850. Soon, the Chicago & Great Eastern Railroad contracted with Scherer to build railroad beds between Richmond, Indiana, and Chicago as superintendent of construction. He also wore many other hats, including as a farmer and a real estate salesperson.

Of the approximate 25 families living within town boundaries at its beginning, the majority were German Catholic. They would be charter members of St. Michael the Archangel Catholic Church built on land donated by Scherer. Completed in the 1870s, it is seen as a town centerpiece to this day. By then the first school and post office were established, yet the town remained a relatively small farming settlement with typical rural character for decades.

Another significant date is September 5, 1911. This is the date when Schererville was officially incorporated as an Indiana town. The incorporating committee was voted in as the first town board. Regardless of which date is celebrated, Schererville itself is something to applaud. The town fathers could hardly have imagined it would one day boast a population of over 29,000.

When Nicholas Scherer, a German immigrant, first came to the northwest Indiana region, he made his home in St. John. During his time in the area, he worked in several different capacities, from farming and construction to administrator of lands for the State of Indiana under the Federal Swamp Land Act of 1850. As work progressed on the construction of ditches that would transform the area's swampland into solid soil, Scherer purchased sufficient acreage from Aaron Hart and had the town recorded and platted on April 10, 1866. Scherer and Hart had much in common. Both made contributions of labor to transform that landscape into acreage on which it would be possible and practical to live, work, and farm. Hart named "his" town after his wife's family name of Dyer. Schererville was named using the Scherer family name. Today, both towns along with nearby St. John compose what has become known as the Tri-Town area of Lake County.

Time has faded this photograph of the Scherer house, in which founder Nicholas Scherer and his wife, Frances, lived and raised their children. Still standing in its original location at 33 East Wilhelm Street, it is now owned by the Town of Schererville. Plans are currently in the works to restore the home inside and out, bringing it to its former glory. Renovations will include structural reinforcement and cosmetic improvements. There will be an effort to furnish the house with period furniture and accoutrements, bringing history alive. The Schererville Historical Society, currently located in the town government center complex, plans to move into the home of its founder. "These projects take a lot of time, research and money, along with the work of good volunteers," said Janice Malinowski, former clerk-treasurer who is spearheading the project for grant applications, fundraising, and total restoration.

Classic photographs such as this one cry out to be shared over and over. It was discovered in a German language book written in 1902. These five gentlemen are, from left to right, Heinrich Schulte, Bernard Schulte, Johann Grimmer, Mathias Helfen, and Nicholas Scherer, the town founder. Each of the men, except for Schulte, has lifted his left arm across his chest to present a stern and somber pose. Their homeland in Europe was probably a distant memory at the time this was taken. For many settlers, it was unlikely they would ever return to the countries where they were born. As they posed here in their new land in America called Schererville, Indiana, they had to know that all the work necessary to create a familiar community life was ahead of them. Despite the challenges they had already experienced and those that were on the horizon, they looked fearless and determined.

These gentlemen are identified only by their first initials and last names. From left to right are N. Schafer, J. Treinen, K. Schubbert, N. Rohrman, J. Maas, and J. Scholl. These family names have endured for generations within the town boundaries. It is important to note that many of these old photographs offer no clue as to the livelihood of the men shown. A farmer only dressed as a farmer while farming, a blacksmith only looked like a smithy when he was doing his hard work, and a gas station mechanic was only in uniform when he worked on engines or pumped gasoline. On Sundays, there was no distinction in dress between a business owner and his employees. A ditchdigger looked equally as prosperous as a hotel owner. Everyone dressed in their finest as a show of respect on the Lord's day.

Notes indicate this picture of the main road in town was taken around 1910. Today's Joliet Street is not only wider but higher, and of course, it is paved. It was an interesting and somewhat challenging journey from dirt road to paved street, eventually adding sewers, sidewalks, and curbs. The prospect of those changes caused an uproar since, to accomplish some of them, several structures had to be moved, and property owners feared that many expenses would be passed on to them. In the memorial book *History of the Crossroads*, written in part by historian Rich Jonas for the 125th anniversary of the town, it is stated that "town minutes are full of disagreements and lawsuits about this." The improvements, which were necessary for the Lincoln Highway project, were finally completed. The Lincoln Highway routing through Schererville helped nudge the town firmly in the direction of prosperity. Travelers then as now seek out good food, gasoline, and places to stay.

To step inside this store in the Cort's Building at 11 East Joliet Street in downtown Schererville, customers would have to walk up at least eight stairs. This photograph was taken in 1911 when Joliet Street was several feet lower than it is today. With the establishment of the new cross-country Lincoln Highway, the roadbed had to be raised, widened, and paved. Those improvements meant that several buildings on Joliet Street would "lose" their stairs. Some of the buildings would be moved back as much as eight feet from their original positions. A study of the movement of structures on the main street of Schererville makes one understand and appreciate what a gargantuan job it was to construct the Lincoln Highway. Similar changes were likely taking place in cities and towns across the country that were on the path of modernization.

Taken in the 1930s, this photograph captures the work in progress for the making of East US 30. In this picture, the men were delivering a healthy load of straw needed to cure the concrete once it was poured. Elmer Wiler is pictured at left with 19-year-old Charles Govert at right. Available sources differ on the exact years when the paving took place through the Schererville region; some say 1932 to 1934, with a widening in 1935, while others say original construction was 1936 to 1937. One thing on which all sources agree is that this major route brought numerous travelers through the area. For local businesses, it meant an increased demand for supplies and services. One reason the increased traffic was welcome was it spurred development while meeting the needs of those passing through.

In this photograph donated to the Schererville Historical Society by Irene Schweitzer Govert, Elmer Wiler is pictured working on the clearing and preparation of the roadbed that would ultimately become US 30. "Several times since its inception, the route has changed a little to either shorten the distance or improve the roads," according to the Indiana Lincoln Highway Association. They identify the two alignments of the highway in Indiana as the 1913 or original route and the 1928 route, which is as it existed when the national Lincoln Highway Association and the Boy Scouts installed concrete posts and signs marking its path. Over time, the name Lincoln Highway would lose its popularity in some places as the route became known simply as US 30. However, many of the businesses that were there from an earlier time still bear some form of the Lincoln Highway name. National and local historians have done an outstanding job preserving its history. Those historical markers are just one way the annals would remain relevant. The Lincoln Highway Association has a total of 12 state chapters.

In 1922, a supply train was in operation delivering goods vital to the local population. It is seen here during a stop at Hart Street and Lincoln Highway. The location of the train stop could have been an indicator of the future importance of the coast-to-coast highway, serving towns and settlements along its route. Today, countless trucks travel US 30, still known and referred to by many as the Lincoln Highway. It has been improved across the country several times since its origin. In Schererville, as in many towns, the route was completely relocated. Today, it is slightly south of its original cut through the town. Box trucks, vans, and semi tractor-trailers traverse it daily to deliver items of all types to businesses and individuals. The crossroads at the junction of US 30 and US 41 is one of the busiest intersections in the country and has come a long way since the day of supply trains.

Some of the paving and construction work that would create the Lincoln Highway/US 30 was done with what would now be considered rudimentary equipment using simple yet ingenious practices. Nevertheless, the workers would manage the tasks brilliantly. This surveyor is pictured using a pickup truck, a ladder, and a platform to get a bird's-eye view of the construction site for the Lincoln Highway. Looking at this early photograph, it is hard to imagine what an important role the road would play in the evolution of Schererville, as it did for towns and cities from the eastern terminal at Times Square in New York City to the western terminal in San Francisco, California. The highway, which travels through the 12 states of New York, New Jersey, Pennsylvania, Ohio, Indiana, Illinois, Iowa, Nebraska, Wyoming, Utah, Nevada, and California, is quintessentially American.

By the 1950s, the town of Schererville was enjoying a good number of modern conveniences. Many roads in town had been paved and took on a much more contemporary appearance. In this photograph taken in May 1958, the George C. Mason Store, a convenient stop for locals and travelers, is visible. A sign in the window advertises a half-gallon of ice cream for 59¢. It sat proudly on Joliet Street, open to serve locals and passersby. The store was a convenience stop, a forerunner to the 7-Eleven and Zip Foods stores of the future. At the time, small towns would often have a cluster of businesses on one main street that usually included a gas station, convenience store, coffee shop or restaurant, and souvenir shop. Business was lucrative, as towns along the highway route were often distanced from each other. Travelers would be anxious to stop and satisfy their needs, not knowing the time or distance before the next opportunity would present itself.

Known as Miller's Tavern, 21 East Joliet Street has changed hands multiple times since the early 1900s, eventually becoming Greg's Place, a popular local tavern and eatery today. The exterior has been altered with modernization, but the spirit of the location remains the same. Newest proprietor Greg Cvitkovich can often be seen talking with patrons, likely in the same manner the original owner did over a century ago.

In the 1930s, Pete Redar was the town marshal. He is seen here posing on Joliet Street, which was Lincoln Highway/US 30. (The route was ultimately relocated.) Redar became the first chief of police, serving over 37 years. His own history is inexplicably tied to Lincoln Highway when, in 1964, stopped at an intersection, a passing semi slammed into his patrol car. He died from the injuries; he was only 68.

As a builder, the hands of John Mager left their talented mark all over town. He built several homes in the area and put up the original St. Michael the Archangel Catholic Church, which was made of wood. Mager was married to the former Barbara Koerner. She is sitting here on the couple's front porch, pictured with five of their ten children. Mager is on left in front, keeping the horse still for the photographer. The home sits on a solid-looking foundation at the corner of Anna and Joliet Streets. It looks very well constructed and includes a glass-paneled decorative front door.

This school building at the corner of Joliet Street and Austin Avenue was built in the early 1890s, replacing a wooden structure that had previously been in use. In the beginning, students arrived at school by horse-drawn buses. Although it was more than a one-room schoolhouse, Schererville Township School No. 1 was still quite a different experience for the pupils compared to the way today's students move around through wide hallways and expansive classrooms. Schererville Township School No. 1 was torn down in 1941 to make room for the construction of Homan School, which was being built by the Works Progress Administration or WPA, a New Deal agency founded by Pres. Franklin D. Roosevelt. Established in 1935, the WPA employed millions across the country who were hired to complete public works projects and help lift the country out of the Depression.

Before the town of Schererville was platted, some people had already settled in the area. Among them were Nicholas and Susana Hilbrich, who had arrived in 1847. They lived in a log cabin Nicholas built himself, using oak logs that were hewn by hand. Over the years, as the needs of the family changed, the simple cabin was expanded and remodeled. Eventually, there was hardly a trace of Hilbrich's original work, but it was within those walls, nevertheless. Descendants of the Hilbrichs retained ownership of the property into the 21st century. When it was sold, the new owner was considering demolition of the old place. Because the town was interested in preserving the cabin in consideration of its historic value, the new owner agreed to let them have it if they would remove it. To prepare for relocation, the structure was stripped down to its original size by removing room additions. When the siding was pulled back, the original cabin logs were exposed, providing a view of something the early settler Hilbrichs saw every day.

It was on August 8, 2008, when the Hilbrich Log Cabin went on a journey. Inch by inch, foot by foot, the old cabin made its way slowly but surely to its new location in Scherwood Park. On moving day, people stood by along the route not only to get a glimpse of the historic cabin, but also to observe the remarkable skill of relocating it safely.

Backing up for the off-load, one can see how the cabin held together thanks to the work of the movers. Once in place, the shoring would be removed from the walls and the rest of the work would begin. The restoration team included the expertise of Dann Keiser, project engineer of Cornerstone Design; Intensified Wood Restoration; Don Elzinga, Ace Cleaning; and Two Uncles Construction. Work was completed in 2016.

By 1992, a shopping center occupied the northeast section of the crossroads of US 30 and US 41. The site included a modern Amoco station on the spot where Sauzer's Waffle House once fed hungry travelers. Visible in the background is the L-shaped strip mall. The center has frequently changed tenants but remains a busy spot attracting shoppers, anchored by Strack and Van Til Supermarket and Wal-Mart. Outbuildings include restaurants and a variety of other useful shops.

Over time, scenes like this are increasingly rare. This picture of the Seberger barn is one of openness. As Schererville's population exploded, farms began to disappear. Although there were less than 4,000 residents within town boundaries in the 1960s, that number would multiply tremendously before the end of the century. For many years, this was the look of the town, but to newcomers and young people, it is barely recognizable as Schererville.

Two

BUSINESS AND INDUSTRY

Known as the Crossroads of the Nation, this endearing designation for Schererville represents a period in the area's history long before US 30 and US 41 were established. It was not these two US highways but Indian trails that inspired the phrase. Native American inhabitants, mostly Pottawatami, preceded modern-day residents and development. The establishment of their trails was just as vital to their way of life then as paved highways are to people now. The Indian trails running through what is now Schererville converged with the Sauk Trail, the main east-west route connecting the Detroit River in Michigan to the Mississippi River in Illinois.

When the age of automobiles arrived, the Lincoln Highway made its way across the nation from New York to San Francisco and helped put Schererville and its main street on the modern-day map. The junction of US 30 and US 41 encouraged and hastened the establishment of new businesses, all of which would help Schererville develop and expand for years to come. As the town continued to populate, other businesses moved in to set up shop. Existing businesses would also benefit from the boost in traffic. By the time the town of Schererville became widely recognized as a regional crossroads, its population was well on the rise.

Based on the strong foundation of their beginnings, businesses such as Teibel's Restaurant, established in 1929, are still thriving today. On the north side of town on Kennedy Avenue and nearby, a light industrial section developed, including businesses such as Midwest Pipe Coating, the Progress Group, and Kennedy Metal Products. In response, the Schererville Chamber of Commerce incorporated nearly 60 years ago to do its part in promoting economic development. There are over 950 licensed businesses in town now, according to code enforcer Sam Decero.

When Schererville began, it was a simple farming settlement. Today, little remains of the expansive agricultural fields of the mid-1800s. Many original farms have given way to residential subdivisions, businesses, and industrial development and expansion. The production and exchange of goods and services by the numerous and diverse businesses in town have created a strong, independent community with easily accessible resources.

The lovely woman in front of Mrs. Turner's Café in the old Turner Building is Clara (Doctor) Toweson, who worked inside as a waitress in the 1930s and 1940s. Its fare was likely tempting to travelers staying in the upstairs rooms rented out by the building's owner. The structure saw other tenants over time but was eventually razed to make room for the new town hall.

This structure would undergo several changes during its long life. Michael Grimmer built it and opened a store inside. Customers would arrive on horseback, on foot, and by wagon. Grimmer eventually sold the store that, at one time, housed the post office. Although Grimmer's name would fade in its association with this location, it would be etched into local minds forever when Grimmer Middle School was named in his honor.

Customers would arrive at Gard's General Store to buy a variety of merchandise, groceries, and even coal. The building was also home to the local post office for a time. It was built around 1879 on Schererville's main drag at 38 East Joliet Road, later to become known as Joliet Street. Like many original buildings, changes would affect its position or orientation, and in the 1960s, the building was lifted and turned to face west. It now sits on the east side of Junction Avenue. Over the years, many owners and tenants have made excellent use of the building either as a business or residential location or both. When the town acquired property directly across the street on the west side of Junction Avenue to construct the current town hall, things changed again for the building, but this time not from within. It was the view from the front door that was completely revised. The entire government complex, including the police station and court, is now within view.

Repairman Art Peifer worked for Turner's Amusement Company fixing music machines as well as gambling machines, which were legal at one time. It explains in *Schererville Through the Years* that the phone number ran through the only local exchange—Dyer. In the 1930s, not many people had the luxury of a telephone and often had to trek some distance to make a call.

From 1945 to 1951, Fath Feed Store was in operation. Spud Mercer is leaning on the doorjamb while Robert Fath poses in front. Fath's store was near the old Turner Building, which, along with other structures, burned down in 1928. But numerous buildings from that era still survive. Schererville businesspeople, residents, and officials have consistently exhibited a desire to maintain original charm while making improvements.

The town's millinery shop was operated in this structure at 30 West Joliet Street. It was a thriving business in its time when nearly every woman in the country wore a hat in public. Millinery is the art of making hats, but historically, the town milliner would also offer other items, including shifts and shirts, neckerchiefs, and more. There are still milliners today who likely undergo a certain amount of training before billing themselves as such. Hats remained hugely popular for men and women through the end of the 1950s. The American hat industry suffered a lack of demand and a downturn in popularity in the early 1960s when the new, young Pres. John F. Kennedy was more often seen and photographed without one. It was a surprising new look at the time.

The John L. Thiel family of Crown Point, Indiana, included his wife, the former Frances Dahlkamp, and their daughter Clara when they relocated and settled in Schererville in 1876. He became the "village smithy," or town blacksmith. In Schererville, the Thiel family would expand to include four more daughters and seven sons: Frances, Kate, John H., Joseph, Lena, Susan, George, William, Emil, Nicholas, and Aloysius. Blacksmiths were essential to early settlers, forging metal for various jobs such as making gates, creating grilles and fences, or repairing wagon wheels. Blacksmiths usually had a wide range of knowledge, from the simple to the complex. From left to right in front of the business are Andrew Doctor, Nicholas Thiel, John H. Thiel, and John Berrens. The Thiel family has a presence in the town to this day. Carol Niebling Clark, a cousin to John Thiel, says her mother, Lucille Thiel Niebling, lived her entire life on Joliet Street; Carol remains in town today.

The so-called food stand shown here was named Maye's Lunch after the owner's daughter Mary Jane "Maye" Gerlach, according to historian Art Schweitzer. It was located on US 30 not too far west of US 41. The popularity of such establishments did not just depend on traffic, although that was a big factor in success. But locals would frequent diners, food stands, and restaurants whenever the food was enticing and the price was reasonable, which is not much different than today. Serving pie with ice cream and chocolate malted milk would also be a big draw. Maye is the young lady in the picture sitting on one of the stools.

Sauzer's Waffle Shop served some of the heartiest and tastiest breakfasts in the area. It not only fed hungry locals, but the restaurant was open 24 hours, especially for the convenience of travelers and truckers on the main routes. Located at the northeast corner of the crossroads of US 30 and US 41, if one journeyed on either of these east-west or north-south routes through Lake County, Indiana, they would pass the Sauzer's Waffle Shop. Inside, postcards featuring the restaurant welcome patrons to visit the owner's other enterprise, Sauzer's Kiddieland Amusement Park, less than a half-mile west on US 30. On that same corner where the Sauzer's Waffle Shop once sat are several businesses, a gas station, and various restaurants. Behind them is an L-shaped strip mall anchored by national chain Wal-Mart on one end and locally owned Strack and Van Til Supermarket on the other.

According to studies, independent restaurants and small chains that make it past the challenging first few years in business have the potential to thrive. But not many could have imagined that when brothers Martin and Stephen Teibel opened their place in 1929, Teibel's Family Restaurant would continue serving dinners well into the next century. Originally, the eatery promoted its delicious fried chicken, but the menu would expand over the years to include much more. Teibel's would also gain acclaim for its boned and buttered perch and enjoy renown across the entire Midwest. It has been at the same crossroads location at the southeast corner of US 30 and US 41 since the beginning, and it is still owned and operated by the Teibel family. From a 12-seat diner to today's restaurant, which includes a banquet hall, dining room, and the café, Teibel's can accommodate over 600 diners at the same time.

Ed Peifer is pictured here in front of Smiling Service Station. It was located at the southeast corner of Joliet Street and Cline Avenue. The station was in operation for about 10 years until 1935. During that period, another photograph clearly shows a sign in the window advertising the price of gas at 16¢ per gallon. Many people today do not know what a "service station" is, even though they may use the term. It was a place not only for refueling one's car, but it was where people went for an oil change, to buy or change tires, or to have their engine repaired or worked on. The men who worked there wore uniforms and hats. Usually, a rubber hose ran across the pavement that cars would cross, which would trigger a bell inside, indicating a customer had arrived, in case they had not seen them. The uniformed attendant would run out, pump the gas, check the oil, and wash the windshield. It was the true definition of service.

In the early 1950s, passersby heading west on US 30 would have seen this idyllic scene soon after crossing US 41. But that would soon change when development began to create Kiddieland Amusement Park. This quiet strip of frontage land and the attached acreage were transformed into one of the area's leading attractions, drawing visitors from near and far for years to come.

Kiddieland was owned and operated by the Sauzer family and was a town attraction for decades. As people drove by on US 30, they could hear the shrieks of joy from children riding the roller coaster or the delightful Ferris wheel. The fair-like atmosphere was a destination for many people, while passersby were often lured inside by the sights and sounds to enjoy a day full of fun.

Pony rides became a featured major attraction at Kiddieland. Safely accompanied by adults, children would be treated to a ride around the specially fenced area. On the right, one can see the tracks for the park's train, which was another thrill for youngsters and adults alike, especially those too young or too shy to ride the roller coaster or Ferris wheel. In addition to games and other rides, there were paddleboats on the pond. The park was opened and operated by Frank Sauzer. Later on, it was his son Frank Jr. who managed it along with his family. Today, most of the former park's land is occupied by the Lakewood Estates development of townhomes and duplexes. A lot of today's Lakewood residents once strolled through Kiddieland on ground that is now part of their own back and front yards.

As times changed, so did Schererville's iconic amusement park. With the town experiencing growing pains, land that offered the potential for the development of more homes and businesses was highly coveted. Growing demand for property continued to intensify, and the area in and around the Kiddieland attractions was listed for sale. The park closed in 1993. Soon, a public auction took place, and the amusements disappeared piece by piece. Before the end of the 20th century, the land would be cleared of all signs of what once was. The joyful sounds of children on rides were replaced with the whirr of heavy equipment, bringing a lot of change with it. Today, the site contains numerous businesses and residential properties.

Once a town of tiny inns and sleeping rooms, Schererville has attracted several national brand hotels in the last few decades. For years, the Radiant Motel offered air-conditioned rooms within walking distance of shopping, restaurants, and Kiddieland. It is still open today in the same location at 1026 West US 30 but under new ownership as the Rosewood Inn. The Staybridge Inn and Suites sit directly across from the Holiday Inn Express and Suites, both conveniently located just off US 30. Also nearby is the Hampton Inn and Suites on US 41, and east of there is the Best Western Crossroads Inn. Throughout town, several other motel choices include the Comfort Inn and the Hometown Inn and Suites all offering beds to weary travelers. In almost all cases, a great eating place is within walking distance. (Above, photograph by Ray Radoja.)

Driving south on Kennedy Avenue from neighboring Highland, one will travel first through Schererville's light industrial district before reaching downtown or many of its residences. Near the Highland/Schererville border are several buildings positioned neatly in a row. They have attracted a variety of businesses, mostly locally owned, offering a diverse selection of goods and services. This development and others help keep the town of Schererville viable. (Photograph by Ray Radoja.)

This enormous structure is part of the Progress Group, locally owned and operated by the Desancic family. The group provides pump repair, machining services, and turbine repair and rebuild, among other things. Its services have reached across the country, but Progress Group predominately does work for industrial companies located in the Midwest. (Photograph by Ray Radoja.)

Midwest Pipe Coating is on the east side of Kennedy Avenue and continues around the corner down Junction Avenue. In addition to the services the company provides at the long-standing business, it touts the convenience of its location. "We are located in Northwest Indiana within 25 miles of both the Port of Indiana-Burns Harbor and the Port of Chicago. Canadian National handles our on-site rail service. Our location offers easy access to Interstate 80/94, U.S. 41 and U.S. 30," it states on their website. That is a beautiful description of the accessibility of Schererville and is part of what makes the town so attractive to all types of businesses and industries. (Both photographs by Ray Radoja.)

This is the view looking north from the intersection of Junction and Kennedy Avenues. Once a quiet curve in the road, even somewhat lonely, it is now very well-traveled with a three-way stop. All the businesses along this stretch keep the area well-maintained. (Photograph by Ray Radoja.)

Now just a dusty pull-off at the dead-end/south end of the intersection of Kennedy and Junction Avenues, one must go east and through town to get to the rest of Kennedy Avenue as it continues. On the drawing board for years, plans are currently underway to extend Kennedy Avenue south to US 30. Town manager Bob Volkmann anticipates the project's first phase will begin in 2023. (Photograph by Ray Radoja.)

It is a great day when one can spend it out in the open air, and Scherwood Golf offers some of the prettiest views of open land left in town. The Ted Locke–designed course was founded by Bill Christenson. According to the website, the inaugural round was played in September 1967. The honored foursome included John Whitaker, a sportswriter for the *Times* (formerly known as the *Hammond Times*); Malcolm Benjamin, who worked at the course; Gene Pettit, who was a partner; and Marvin Hanson, who served as course superintendent. In 1979, Hanson along with his wife, Eileen, purchased the golf property. Since its early beginnings, Scherwood has undergone some expansion and modification. In addition to the 18-hole regulation course, it now includes a nine-hole executive course, putting greens, and a driving range. Some of the beautiful Greens of Scherwood townhomes have the added benefits of being able to watch golfers, enjoy a view overlooking a pond, and live in a convenient location near downtown Schererville. (Photograph by Ray Radoja.)

While this picture was taken on a cold November day, it is not likely one will find this many open parking spaces when it is golf weather. Scherwood Golf was developed adjacent to the original Scherwood Club, which was put up by Bill Christenson in the 1950s. At the club, members had access to an Olympic-sized swimming pool and clubhouse. In addition to banquets, parties, and other member events, there were popular weekly dances during summers in the 1960s. Teenagers from across the region would flock to fill the clubhouse and listen to the dance music of area bands. The Scherwood Club was on nine acres that were ultimately sold to the Town of Schererville in 2004. The banquet building was razed in 2005, and the Schererville Community Center fills the spot where many activities are hosted by the parks and recreation department. The vacant property in front on Joliet Street is now Scherwood Park. Behind the community center, the historic Hilbrich Log Cabin, dating from the 1840s, sits in its new location where it was restored and is preserved. (Photograph by Ray Radoja.)

This kind of traffic would have been unimaginable to early settlers when Schererville's downtown was in its first stages of development. Looking east on Joliet Street, this photograph was taken before business hours on a Tuesday morning. It demonstrates the constant comings and goings of cars driving to and through the business district. Before US 30 was relocated south about a half-mile, there would have been even more cars on the original route. For a while, it seemed as if downtowns might be a thing of the past in America. The development of shopping centers in the 1950s and later enclosed malls took many businesses away from downtown main streets throughout the country. More people owned cars, and the shortage of parking spaces in older business districts was also a drawback. Now, downtowns seem to be making a comeback with the trend to shop local. (Photograph by Ray Radoja.)

Three

COMMUNITY

When a group of people is living in the same geographic area, they are referred to as a community. The definition of the word "community" also includes the feelings of fellowship with others. Some sources cite the origin of the word as from the old French *comunete*, which carries a third definition: reinforced by its source. All of these describe the town of Schererville.

As part of the community, Schererville residents and business owners enjoy a general feeling of belonging shared through their common connection to the town. Each has a vested interest in the maintenance and betterment of the community, regardless of how long they have been here. Whether anyone realizes it or not, that type of attachment began way back when the first section of land was carved out and given the name Schererville by its founder, Nicholas Scherer. The town's name is often misspelled and mispronounced: Shareville, Shearville, Shearerville, and other incorrect variations. Those mistakes provide just one more reason to know the town's history and celebrate Scherer's foresight.

While there is a sense of gratitude to Scherer, he is certainly not singularly responsible for the success of the town. Credit must also go to the thousands who have come after him doing their part to perpetuate all that is great about living here. As the town's history is passed down, some homage goes to Scherer. More importantly, town residents share a responsibility to keep the town vibrant by doing what they can, no matter how large or small, to beautify and maintain this little patch of ground.

Lastly, a common location and feelings of fellowship are not the only things that comprise the sense of community. More than any other definition, community means people. This town would not be what it is today were it not for the hard work and sacrifice of both the early settlers and its current residents.

World War I cost millions their lives. The war began July 28, 1914, about a month after young Gavrilo Princip assassinated Austrian archduke Franz Ferdinand in Sarajevo on St. Vitus Day or Vidovdan, June 28, 1914. Princip was a Bosnian Serb who was not quite 20 years old at the time. His mission was to bring down Austro-Hungarian rule in the Balkans and unite the South Slav people into one nation, but instead, it started a war. He was apprehended and sentenced to prison for the deed. The United States joined the Allies against the Central Powers of Germany, Austria-Hungary, and Turkey in 1917. Young soldiers, such as this handsome man, were whisked off across the Atlantic to fight for freedom. As for Princip, he took ill in prison with what is presumed to have been tuberculosis and died in a hospital in 1918. He never saw the fulfillment of his dream of a united South Slav nation. The Kingdom of Serbs, Croats, and Slovenes was formed on December 1, 1918, months after his death.

Thousands of miles from the little town of Schererville, Indiana, the war to end all wars was underway. The conflict reached out and touched people who lived in this little farming community just as it did in cities and towns across the entire country. This photograph is of Peter Reiplinger, who registered for the military and served during World War I. The Reiplinger family name has deep roots in Schererville. Reiplinger's Garage and Shell Station once occupied the spot at Joliet Street and US 30, where the old historic Lincoln Highway and the new US 30 converge. The location is now home to Pete's RV Sales and Service. In this photograph of Reiplinger, one cannot help but wonder what was on the mind of the young man. Dashing and handsome with his parted, neatly combed hair and in his uniform, he was of a certain age when young men think of themselves as invincible.

Then came World War II. Art Miller is pictured here on a bright, sunny day in front of the home of his parents, Lawrence and Carrie Miller, on Wilhelm Street. Everywhere across America, the thought of sending sons and daughters was considered a patriotic duty. Young men and women proudly volunteered to serve their country and fight for the freedoms of others.

Two decades after World War I, Americans were drawn into World War II when war on Japan was declared within days of the bombing of Pearl Harbor, Oahu, Hawaii, on December 7, 1941. The call to serve was bravely answered by America's sons and daughters. On June 7, 1942, six months to the day after the bombing of Pearl Harbor, Ervin "Pinsky" Bohling poses as he prepares to leave Schererville and report for duty.

This group of five men is identified with only four names: Willie Doctor, Jack Seibert, Bob Stephen, and Addie Schweitzer. Cars and uniforms clearly show this photograph was taken in the World War II era. The men may have been home on leave or were celebrating the end of the war. During that decade, there were no mobile phones with FaceTime nor had anyone heard of the Internet. Even landline phones were not that common. When a fellow left for war, he was almost entirely dependent on the mail. Letters from home were nearly as important as food and water to those far away. Money was not plentiful either. In 1944, for instance, an Army private was making about $50 a month, which is about $850 in today's money. Although Pres. Franklin D. Roosevelt instituted the draft in 1940, approximately two million men volunteered to serve in branches of the armed forces during World War II.

Baseball was still America's favorite pastime when this team photograph was taken in 1960. The Schererville Town League began in September 1954 thanks to Herb Govert, Al Hanson, Al Schreiber, and Al Peifer, whose leadership made it happen. They played ball on the land at US 30 and Anna Street right by St. Michael the Archangel Catholic Church. This Schererville team is anchored by coach Bill Willer, back left; Mike Kozuch, center; and manager Abe Bryant,

right. The players are, from left to right, (first row) Bruce Mokate, Rusty Reeder, Buddy Darnell, Charlie Atcher, Bill Schweitzer, Bill Willer, Ken Robinson, and Ivan Zimmer; (second row) Ron Austgen, Jerry Hancock, John Larimer, Bob Crider, and Phil Govert. Other players who were not pictured are Jim Greybill and Pat Gibson.

As the number of players and teams registering grew, a minor league was established. A second team was entered into the South Suburban Babe Ruth League. This is a picture of the 1961 championship Schererville Tigers. From left to right are (first row) Bill Schweitzer, Chuck Grummer, Joe Furjanic, Larry Kozuch, Charlie Atcher, Glen Keilman, and Mickey Schau; (second row) coach Bill Willer, Jerry Jung, Bill Willer, Dave Garrett, Jim Adams, Ken Robinson, Ron Austgen, Ivan

Zimmer, Jerry Hancock, and manager Abe Bryant. From the original four teams—the Sauzer Cards, the Teibel Cubs, the Watts Hardware Sox, and the Farm Bureau Yankees—until now, the league has moved around to other fields due to its size. Hundreds participate every year. Although football, hockey, soccer, and volleyball enjoy increased popularity, baseball is still America's favorite pastime, especially in Schererville.

Life was not as easy as it appears in this photograph of Peter Cope and his wife, Carrie. Taken in 1922, likely on a Sunday afternoon judging by their fine clothing, Peter served as the town's second marshal from 1925 to 1927. Long, hard work was the norm for everyone. Men often worked long days of 12 hours or more on the job or in the field and usually for six days a week. While the men normally spent daytime hours working, women's work was unending. Almost everything was done by hand. Sweeping was done with a broom and dustpan; meals were cooked from scratch, including bread; a washtub with wringer rolls was a luxury; and wet clothes were hung outside to dry. Suits were brushed and not sent to the cleaners. Ironing was tedious, sprinkled with water to moisten fabric and remove wrinkles. Baby food was mashed up from table foods; only cloth diapers were used. Sunday was usually a day of worship and rest, but women still prepared the meals and cleaned the kitchen afterward.

Two other pictures of the lovely corner house built in 1905 are shown here. The Copes are on right with Guy Dunfee Sr., standing on the left. Ninety years after its construction at 36 East Wilhelm Street, a more modern picture was taken (below). The owners were identified as the Zahler family. The home is easily identifiable by the pretty attic window above the front porch in all the photographs. By 1995, the addition of bushes, trees, and hanging baskets of flowers enhanced the home. Evergreens offered privacy to the very porch where the old settlers once posed. At right in the 1995 picture is the American flag. A wooden figure of Uncle Sam is waiting by the front door. It is a most welcoming American scene, symbolizing Schererville then and now.

Community is all about pitching in. It is the original teamwork. Residents live together, work together, and have fun together. It is the town of Schererville that connects them. The Schererville Chamber of Commerce sponsors a corn roast each year. The tradition has spanned six decades and takes place every year in Redar Park. There are food vendors, craft vendors, retail booths, and live entertainment, not to mention a big favorite of the over-21 crowd—the beer garden. The biggest food attraction of the day is the corn on the cob. The corn roast is usually open from 4:00 p.m. to 8:00 p.m., but the beer garden stays hopping later into the evening. The low admission cost includes soda, water, and all-you-can-eat corn, which explains the sign, "A maximum of four corn at a time, please. This will help us serve all our neighbors equally!" In this scene, several volunteers are chipping in to prepare the tasty ears.

As of 2021, Indiana ranks fifth among all corn-producing states in the United States. Although Schererville is no longer an agricultural town, as proud Hoosiers, it recognizes that the state of Indiana is part of the heartland where most of the corn in the country is produced. That fact could have been the idea behind having an annual corn roast sponsored by the business community through its chamber of commerce. Judging by the smiles in this picture, it is more likely the delicious taste of fresh, locally grown corn on the cob. What better reason or excuse to arrange a mini-festival with attractions than a good, hot ear of buttery corn? In town, the local chamber of commerce does more than just serve businesses or sponsor a corn roast. It keeps people in the community informed and connected while having a deliciously good time.

Often seen during town festivals and picnics are exciting and entertaining performances by dance and cheer groups from the Lake Central Community Schools. At Lake Central High School, which encompasses students from St. John, Dyer, and Schererville, the Centralettes have earned some top awards, such as the National Dance Association Jazz Championship. They were also state finalists in the hip-hop category. In 2015, they traveled to Orlando, Florida, where they competed at the Hard Rock at Universal Studios. Another time the dancers performed at the NBA Chicago Bulls game. Their strong commitment to long, hard hours of practice has enabled them to achieve some of the highest rankings at regional, state, and national competitions over the years. Amazing choreography, outstanding coaching, and parental support are big parts of their road to high achievements. Despite their incredible success, they have always found time to remember their hometowns and perform locally.

At the Schererville Chamber of Commerce Corn Roast in 2006, there were a lot of live performances. These young ladies in their Force uniforms entertained the crowd on the pavilion stage in Redar Park. From a one-room schoolhouse that surely did not teach dance or cheer, the Lake Central system is awesome in size. There are three middle schools that feed into the enrollment at Lake Central High School. Kahler Middle School is in Dyer, Clark Middle School is in St. John, and Grimmer Middle School is in Schererville. With the sheer number of total residents in the Tri-Town area, school enrollment is higher today than the total population of Schererville was in 1966, when the town was celebrating its centennial. There is no shortage of organized school-associated groups willing to perform at town picnics and other events. Such appearances and participation contribute to the overall atmosphere of community, binding the residents to the schools even if they have no schoolchildren in their families.

Corn is not the only item in demand at the corn roast. Here is the sausage and sauerkraut booth. A serving of corn would probably be included on demand. For certain people who have attended these and other similar past events, it probably only takes a whiff of roasting corn or the sight of hats and aprons like these to conjure up memories of fun summer days at Redar Park.

People line up early for town parades. During the Celebrate Schererville Festival, organizations, businesses, elected officials, and others decorate floats to parade down Joliet Street. Schools participate with their bands and cheerleaders and dancers, all creating a festive day. This photograph was taken in 1992 when the railroad track still crossed Joliet Street near Junction Avenue.

On June 21, 2006, these two young people were crowned Little Mr. Schererville and Little Miss Schererville. Their petite sizes were not wide enough to display the full titles on their decorative ribbons. But the crowns on their heads and the smiles on their faces were all that was needed for everyone to see they were bursting with pride to be honored. The crowning took place at the annual Celebrate Schererville Festival. People from throughout town and across the region look forward to the event each year with carnival rides, games, live entertainment, vendors of goods and good foods, and, of course, the beer garden, including craft beers. In addition to what goes on at the Redar Park site Wednesday through Sunday, the parade takes place on Saturday. It is one of the highlights of summer in town.

This appears to be a family of four sitting in the grass on the Peter Kuhn farm. They are identified as Teresa, Helen, Mary, and Rose. The farmhouse, barn, and property are long gone. In their places today sit the LeJardin Condominiums between Joliet Street; the original Lincoln Highway; and US 30, the modern Lincoln Highway. Now, many families enjoy sun-splashed summer afternoons at the very same location. Peter Kuhn was one of the area's original settlers, having arrived in or around 1868 when he was just a young lad of 11 years old. He worked with Aaron Hart driving oxen pulling plows to level ground for the first road right-of-way that is now US 41. Married to Anna Thomas in 1887, the Kuhns had 12 children. Peter passed away in 1932, while Anna passed away in 1952.

Around 1935, the Doffin family gathered at their family homestead to take this treasured keepsake photograph in front of their porch. From left to right are (seated) Wilhelm Doffin, Clara Doffin Popp, Nicholas Doffin Sr., Agnes Gerlach Doffin, Henry Doffin, and Agnes Doffin Scheidt; (standing) Elizabeth Doffin Rettig, Frank Doffin, Frances Doffin Kreiter, Alfred Doffin, Margaret Doffin Hurst, Nicholas Doffin Jr., and Matilda Doffin Geisen. Large families were quite common at the time. As a result, a single surname can leave a widespread and indelible mark on a community and its surrounding areas as children marry and have children of their own and so on. This photograph is a fine example of pictures taken in the 1930s and is very common in cities and towns throughout the country. Big family gatherings often ended in front of a camera lens, in front of the family home, celebrating togetherness.

From 1936 until 1966, this was the Mel Fath home in Schererville. The picture of these children who appear to be having a great time playing together was taken in 1939. This was a time when people would gather around the radio to listen for word from Pres. Franklin D. Roosevelt on the possibility that America would join the forces already at war in Europe. It was also a time when little girls, and women for that matter, almost exclusively wore dresses whether they were at work, at school, relaxing, or at play. Pants for women soon gained popularity in the 1940s as more women entered the workplace since so many men were away at war. It was a change of style based on practicality, not a statement of equality as it later became.

George Schumacher is pictured here with these lovely ladies who are part of the Schumacher family. When their names changed through marriage, they became Mathilda Stephen, Clara Maginot, Theresa Trinen, Alvina Hammer, and Lauretta Schweitzer. The identification was made by historian Art Schweitzer who did not record the year or his precise connection to the family.

Posing for the camera here is Vernon Schweitzer at left. Vernon's young son Jimmie is seated on his great-grandfather's lap; the eldest is Peter Schweitzer. John Schweitzer is seated at right. Photographs such as these, with four generations represented, become family treasures.

Schererville's downtown had a drastically different look in the 1930s. Turner's gas station, where they sold Deep Rock gas and motor oil, sat at 18 East Joliet Street. Pictured is Bob Britton ready to pump gas, check oil, and give change for a cash payment from his waistline coin dispenser. That level of service and method of payment would begin to phase out a few decades later. The station closed in the 1940s. During its heyday, customers came from across the United States making their way on the original transcontinental Lincoln Highway. Today's stations are almost entirely self-serve. In addition to gas, one can buy lottery tickets, get lunch, and have the car washed, to name a few choices. When Bob Britton worked here, he was the one who pumped the gas, there was no state lottery, and very few, if any, food selections were inside. They were called service stations for good reasons. Customers could remain in their car while someone like Bob provided all the services required for them to continue along their way.

These two couples are posed on the steps of St. Michael the Archangel Catholic Church. The brides are absolutely beautiful in their knee-length gowns of silk and lace. The Roaring Twenties made beaded gowns and Flapper styles with drop waists extremely popular. Exposing the calf was a daring new fashion concept for ladies. Hemlines are often good time lines.

Taken in front of Teibel's in the 1930s, this picture includes some of the Teibel family owners. From left to right are (first row) Steve Teibel, Ed Blankenberg, and Martin Teibel; (second row) unidentified; Mary Pasel Redar; unidentified; Helen Stevens Huseman; Emma Schmidt Redar, wife of Marshal Pete Redar; and Marie Reybicki Teibel.

During the centennial celebration, which took place from June 29 through July 4, 1966, many participating men and women dressed in period clothing to help characterize the occasion. A lot of men grew beards and wore pins declaring them a Brother of the Brush. The women dressed in garments representing the 1860s and were declared Centennial Belles. They were also honored with pins. It was an exciting time in town. The population was on a continued upward scale, and development was spreading all over the area. In comparison to some of the northern cities of Lake County, Schererville still seemed like a "little farm town." But there was no doubt about the rate of and potential for growth. The 2020 US Census report indicates the town has swelled to 29,613 residents, which was after more land was incorporated. (Photograph by Ray Radoja.)

Frank Sauzer Sr. is striking in his neatly trimmed beard and Kentucky colonel tie. Although Frank and Edna Sauzer were not among the earliest settlers in the area, they arrived back in 1941 and almost immediately established Sauzer's Waffle Shop. It remained in operation until 1990. As late as 1966, when the town marked its first 100 years, Schererville was still considered a small community. But the Sauzers were a huge part of it. Frank and Edna did more than operate the restaurant. They also developed and opened Sauzer's Kiddieland not far from the waffle shop about a half-mile west on US 30. For many region residents, all they knew of Schererville was Teibel's, the Scherwood Club, Sauzer's Waffle Shop, and Sauzer's Kiddieland. As Schererville continued to grow, these early businesses had a strong foothold and served travelers, truckers, fun-seekers, and locals for decades. Frank Jr. and his wife, Jane, continued the work of Frank and Edna for many years after this picture was taken.

It seems rather fitting that the Schererville Community Center occupies the land that once was the site of a private club for members and their guests only. Today, the community center is open to all and hosts a wide variety of events for the public throughout the calendar year. Located at 500 East Joliet Street off Scherwood Greens Drive, the multipurpose facility also serves surrounding communities. The center is available for rent. There are 12,500 square feet inside the building, which also includes the park department offices. Several attractive rooms can accommodate anywhere from a small gathering to over 280 people at a time comfortably. There are convenient fitness and wellness programs geared to adults. Popular activities such as Zumba, Yoga, and Pilates are healthy options. In addition to what takes place at the center, the parks department also offers adult group golf lessons, adult softball leagues, and more. From seasonal craft shows to Santa's annual arrival in town, the community center remains one of Schererville's most popular places. (Photograph by Ray Radoja.)

Four

GOVERNMENT AND MORE

While the people who live in town are the face of Schererville, the community is managed by multiple layers of government constantly working to provide services, maintain order and safety, offer recreation, make improvements, and preserve beautification, just to name a few of the responsibilities. The State of Indiana, County of Lake, and St. John Township all have a handful of responsibilities in Schererville. But it is the local town government that has the highest visibility and meets immediate needs.

Within the town are the planning and building department, public works, parks and recreation, animal control, police and fire departments, and the town court. There are also the clerk-treasurer's staff and the Southcom PSAP for 9-1-1 assistance. The 2022 town council, consisting of Robin Arvanitis, Kevin Connelly, Rob Guetzloff, Caleb Johnson, and Tom Schmitt, is responsible for administration in the five wards and throughout the town as a whole. Council members also have designated assignments on the utility and waterworks boards and the redevelopment commission. The board of safety, overlooking the fire and police departments, and park board consist of citizen appointments; Judge Randy Wyllie sits on the bench of the town court; and Michael Troxell serves as clerk-treasurer.

The council continually reevaluates what it takes to keep Schererville running efficiently. Collectively, town administration, departments, and employees perform their duties at a level above assigned duties. "We will keep doing all we can to help make Schererville a wonderful town to call home," is the statement on schererville.org. Those words reflect the investment of town fathers and the commitment of those in charge today.

It was June 1914 when the Schererville Volunteer Fire Department was first organized at a meeting of the town board. There were 25 volunteers under the leadership of Fred Henderlong, who was appointed chief. This early photograph shows a ladder truck purchased in 1922 and housed at the first fire station.

By 1930, the original building looked more like an official fire station. John Thiel, the town blacksmith and a volunteer fireman, is shown standing near the fire truck. Police chief Pete Redar is at right. The building had been painted, other improvements were made, and a sign was mounted declaring it the home of the fire department.

Taken in 1939, Andy Doctor is seen seated at the steering wheel. Standing near the searchlight on the left is William Schiesser. Continuing clockwise are Clarence Schafer, John Thiel Sr., Joe Zimmer, Joe Risch, Herbert Govert, Joe Schiesser, Mathias Kuhn, Ben Schulte, William Redar, Frank Place, Louie Meter, Al Govert, John Thiel Jr., Clarence Klassen, Pete Redar, Michael Kuhn, Al Peifer, Earl Toweson, and Joe Homan. Many of the family names in this list may seem familiar, even to some of Schererville's newest residents, as they can be seen all around town today on business signs, local parks, and schools. Firemen were compensated a dollar for each meeting they attended, a dollar for any call they answered, and a dollar an hour for each hour they were on duty. Those pay rates were first established in 1953, and they remained unchanged for years.

This fire department picture was taken around 1960. From left to right are (first row) Arnold Peifer, Frank Gard, Art Schweitzer, Sylvester Schweitzer, Merl Hammond, George Niebling, John Molson, and Leo Grimmer; (second row) Rev. Timothy Doody, Norb Grimmer, Jack Siebert, Ed Koch (in the truck), Al Peifer, Clarence Schafer, Al Hanson, John Render, Robert Hensley, Robert Adley, and William Schiesser.

Pictured is the fire department in 1991. From left to right are (first row) Steve Neumeier, Mark Semethy, Carmen Mosca, Jerry Bauer, Frank Peters, Jim Watters, Dan Peppin, Ed Kaeser, Terry Sherwood, Bud Darnell, Jerry Balaz, Fred Belligio, Roger Walters, Mike Talbert, and George Turoci; (second row) George Schulp, Jerry Schmitt, Dan Gray, Tom Schweitzer, Jim Schaap, Bill Howe, George Michels, Harvey Lanning, Jim Lesniewski, Gerry Denhartog, Gary Hays, Rich Kramer, John Vought, Jeff Bridegroom, Ed Jasaitis, and Jim Vargo. Nineteen firemen were not pictured.

New equipment, modernization, and expansion are all words associated with the Schererville Fire Department (SFD). From fire trucks to radio alerting systems, the department has continually grown with the town. By 1973, it had expanded to 40 men. Within two years, another fire station was built at the corner of Joliet Street and Cline Avenue. The adjoining unincorporated area of New Elliott had its own facility when its volunteers merged with Schererville's Fire Department in 1977. The number of fire stations serving the community then rose to three. In the meantime, the north end around Plum Creek subdivision was populating quickly, making it apparent another facility would be needed. Station No. 4 was built on Plum Creek Drive. Ambulance services were added, and a fifth station was built on the growing south end of town. Today, the department is very involved at the Tri-Town Safety Village educating schoolchildren on fire safety. In its 100-plus years of history, SFD has had eight fire chiefs: Fred Henderlong, Clarence Schafer, Norbert Fortner, Joseph Govert, Edward Kaeser, George Michels, Joseph Kruzan, and Robert Patterson.

One cannot fight fires without water, and Schererville needed a good source. This well was the first of its kind inside the town. It became operational in 1920 and was located at the original police station, fire station, and town hall, where meetings took place. The source of the well was an underground river. Its power is evident in this display that must have fascinated the youngsters watching.

Standing tall and working constantly for Schererville is this "first of its kind" water tower, proudly displaying the name of the town. Looking a bit like a giant mushroom, it was completed in 1959 by Graver Tank & Manufacturing Company Inc., a business located in East Chicago, Indiana. It remains in service to the town today and serves as a landmark.

In this undated early photograph, Schererville police chief Pete Redar responds to an accident at US 41 and Airport Road. The intersection saw so many problems that Airport Road was eventually closed for safety reasons. Redar was one of the earliest policemen and used his personal vehicle in his official capacity for years.

Another accident response was made in this scene played out in front of Sauzer's Waffle Shop on the northeast corner of the crossroads. The Indiana State Police often lent a hand in Schererville, particularly on the state roads of US 30 and US 41. The Schererville Historical Society dates this to the late 1940s based on the size of Sauzer's, which had not yet been expanded.

At one time, it was not unusual to see police patrolling on horseback. In this picture, Indiana state trooper Lawrence Miller makes his way on his trusty mount, which was provided by the Indiana State Police. Miller was also seen about town in a squad car and was, in fact, the state trooper whose car is pictured at the scene of the accident in front of Sauzer's on the previous page.

Looking like the squad in *Car 54, Where Are You*, this police car was a new 1963 Chevrolet. It was outfitted with a red light on the roof, often called a "cherry," and a siren on the hood. The patrolman on duty in the picture is Bob Florkiewicz. There was an unidentified passenger riding in Car 32 that day as they patrolled around town.

Town and state police were not alone in upholding the law. Stanley Lukasik served as justice of the peace and was often identified as Schererville's local judge. Here, he is confirming the inventory of confiscated gambling machines with Steve Ranich of the Indiana State Police. The pair were matching serial numbers before slating the machines for demolition.

Once slot machines and gambling devices went through the process of confiscation and identification, Justice of the Peace Stanley Lukasik (left) would oversee the final step to destroy them. He is pictured here while someone with a sledgehammer brings down the long arm of the law. The picture was taken in front of the Indiana State Police post, which, at one time, was located on US 30.

By 1960, the Schererville Police had hired more patrolmen. From left are Tom Long, John Stephen, Joe Zimmer, James Westerfield, Gene Wall, Phil Spivak, John Seaman, Pete Redar, and Bob Teegarden. Pete Redar, who served from 1927 to 1964, was the first marshal and later became chief, as did Phil Spivak, who was appointed chief in 1964.

This department photograph was taken in 1991 when Dennis Zagrocki served as chief of police. The continual growth of the department was obvious, and it was expanding in more ways than simply the number of personnel. Officer Friendly and DARE programs were added, the department had its own radio room, women had been added to the department, and there was a K-9 unit.

Squad cars, horses, and walking shoes were not the only means of transportation. This patrolman was making his rounds on a bicycle in August 2006. He is shown near Redar Park in the center of town. Bicycles proved handy to have quick access to areas not easily reached by car. With the number of parks and bike paths in town, it became a great alternative that was also environmentally friendly.

Schererville's police department was the first one in Lake County to have a K-9 or canine unit. In 1975, John Siedelmann and John Wade were the first two officers to be designated as dog handlers. In this picture are Larry Myslywiec and his police dog Boss. Myslywiec could often be seen exercising Boss near the police station.

At one time, the police station had temporary headquarters at AAA Supply Corporation on US 41. This picture was taken in late 1999 showing police chief Daniel Smith at his desk. The temporary quarters were being used while the new police station was under construction. Barely visible through the window and just next to the flagpole outside is the AAA sign.

Being a patrol boy is a job that was taken seriously by young Bill Govert, who distinguished himself at school and was recognized for his work. An award was presented by town marshal Pete Redar in this picture. The police do more than look for criminals or transport prisoners to the county lockup. They have always taken an active interest in the community and are respected by the townspeople.

Schererville has had several post office locations since 1866 when Mathias Meyers was the first postmaster and mail arrived in town by train. From its humble beginnings in a downtown store to its modern facility on Eagle Ridge Drive, the US Postal Service and the employees for zip code 46375 handle the mail with expertise. This 1966 photograph shows an earlier location of the post office on Joliet Street.

The walking mail deliverer in this picture is Edie Govert Adams. She enjoyed a long career with the postal service. During her time there, she moved on from a walking route to a mail truck. Some people still long for the days of the walking mail delivery. That was when people often knew their mail person by name, and the mail person knew their name, too.

During the centennial year of 1966, clerk-treasurer Joe Zimmer (right) was charged with administering the oath of office to newly elected town council members. From left to right are John Dressen, Ralph McColly, and Bob Teegarden. Many of these names were familiar to residents as Schererville was still a relatively small town. Just about everyone was involved, working or volunteering on some level.

In the early 2000s, Schererville Town Council meetings took place in the lower level of an office building on US 30 and US 41 at West Lincoln Highway. Beginning the meeting reciting the Pledge of Allegiance are, from left to right, Councilmen Ed Cook, Michael Troxell, Steve Kil, and John Fladeland, town attorney David M. Austgen, Councilman Rob Guetzloff, and clerk-treasurer Janice Malinowski.

Elected officials are not the only people working for the town. There have always been volunteers and committees doing time-consuming tasks such as planning town anniversaries. Schererville's 1966 Centennial Committee consisted of, from left to right, (first row) Shirley Phillips, Bud Phillips, Marian Britton, Clarence Smith, and Lucille Vance; (second row) Robert Adley, Wallace Michael, Larry Anderson, James Watson, John Dressen Jr., Stan Mastey, and Al Peifer. Not pictured are Ted Plimpton and Celia Adley.

For the 125th town anniversary, volunteers for the committee are, from left to right, (first row) Pat McAllister, Joanne Domsic-Stephen, Mary Jascula, Bonnie Rosenberg, and Patricia Dykstra-Sons; (second row) Gerry Scheub, Smokey Smith, Michael Troxell, Vic Banter, Rich Jonas, and Jim Ikovic. (Absent from the photograph is John Novacich.) The celebration took place at the Illiana Speedway and was complete with rides, games, and a demolition derby.

These young women were the centennial queen and her court who posed during the 1966 celebration. The gowns were the height of fashion at the time, and the ladies were absolutely beautiful. From left to right are Bonnie (Siebert) Wood, Nancy Teibel, Marion (Glosser) Hanson, queen Judy Teibel, Mary Jane (Maye) Gerlach, Evelyn (Redar) Matthews, and Sharon (Keilman) Craven.

Not as sophisticated but certainly as charming are these two youngsters decked out in period clothing for the town's centennial. They are Wendy and Margaret Anderson. The picture serves a dual purpose by giving us the exact dates of the festival: June 29 through July 4. Also learned from the poster is that fireworks went off nightly and there was street dancing and a ladies' ball game during the week's festivities.

Five

SCHOOLS AND
HOUSES OF WORSHIP

When the 1800s settlers arrived, they brought with them a knowledge of how to work the land to sustain their well-being. They began to flourish, focusing on the results of their struggles rather than giving in to them. They were compensated for their diligence with food on the table, a warm and dry place to sleep, and the promise of a continually better life. They lived up to their description as "settlers" as they established their new lives in a new place. Their success took root, and others arrived to follow in their footsteps. Schererville had its true beginning.

In an agricultural settlement, the hard work of farming meant all hands were needed, including the youngest. But the settlers came to two important conclusions that had a hand in changing their priorities. They wanted a church, a place to give thanks, and to organize a school for their children to get some "book-learning."

From the modest one-room schoolhouse in the township to the several schools of the Lake Central system within the town's boundaries today, education was valued as highly as worship and work. The first church, dedicated to St. Michael the Archangel, eventually added its own school, too. Over time, numerous houses of worship were established in town, serving the faithful of the Lutheran, Presbyterian, Baptist, varying Orthodox ethnicities, and others. Islamic centers and mosques and Jewish temples sit within easy access to the town. All of this illustrates the diverse population of the once tiny town of Schererville.

Built in the late 1800s, Schererville Township School No. 1 replaced the original wooden schoolhouse of District No. 1. It would remain in use through 1941, up until the time Homan Elementary School was built to take its place. Students would clamor excitedly to get a horse-drawn ride home; teachers and other staff stood by, watching them board. Adult women wore street-length skirts, while young girls wore fashionable shorter ones baring their ankles.

A view of Schererville Township School No. 1 from the side shows it is not quite as imposing as it appeared from the front. It was actually a simple, sturdy building that served its function within the community. Where once wagonloads of students pulled up in horse-drawn buses, barely visible on right is the new school under construction.

Homan Elementary School was built right next door to Schererville Township School No. 1 at Joliet Street and Austin Avenue. Construction was done by the Works Progress Administration (WPA), a program that left many enduring signs of both work and progress throughout the town of Schererville. Homan has been improved and expanded several times since 1941; the original building had only four classrooms.

In 1993, Michael Troxell was part of a committee working to save the original Schererville Township School No. 2. Efforts to restore the historical structure and preserve it for future generations were successful, enabling others to learn firsthand about Schererville's past. Much of the original material was salvaged for use during the restoration, which was completed in 1994.

One of 12 one-room schoolhouses throughout St. John Township, this deteriorating wooden structure was rescued by well-meaning preservationists. It was located at Old St. John and Nowak Roads and then sold and moved to another location on the east side of Dyer, where it was "found." Today, it sits near the St. John Township Trustee's Office. Volunteers "teach" modern-day fourth graders what the school experience was in the 1800s.

Desks lined neatly in rows, each accommodating two students, comprised a typical scene inside schoolhouses during the 1800s and early 20th century. This one-room schoolhouse known as St. John Township School No. 2 was in use from 1853 to 1907. Its restoration included stocking it with period items that would have been in the school when it was in daily use, such as portraits of Presidents Lincoln and Washington.

Young students gathered in front of the restored schoolhouse to cut the ribbon at its rededication on May 14, 1994. It had taken about nine months to bring it back to life. The first several weeks were spent tediously disassembling and separating reusable wood from boards deemed beyond salvation. Some people questioned the expenditure of effort, time, and money spent on the project, but living history is a treasured asset.

In this more modern picture taken inside the restored schoolhouse are some of the people who were especially happy to see the project undertaken. From left to right are Jim and Kathy (Govert) Dinges; Glen Everly, president of the Dyer Historical Society; Bill Tulley of the St. John Historical Society; and Art Schweitzer, president of the Schererville Historical Society. People today benefit from their hard work keeping history alive.

James H. Watson served as superintendent of schools in Schererville beginning in 1957, and prior to that, he was a principal in the schools. Continuing his career, he was named assistant superintendent of the Lake Central School System in 1967. In January 1978, this elementary school was named in his honor. His daughter Betty Seegers (left) and his wife, Pauline Watson, are shown in front of the sign bearing his name.

Considered a reasonable acquisition price, this structure cost only $75 plus moving expenses. It was then modified to be used as the very first St. Michael School beginning in the early 1890s. It was originally used for religious instruction. It later became a parochial school. An addition was attached that made it possible to accommodate 42 students at one time.

When the wooden building was relocated it sat on a higher foundation. The relocation and expansions in 1901 and 1902 gave St. Michael School an entirely new look. When the next newest St. Michael School was erected, the old wooden structure was sold, dismantled, and some of its wood was used in the construction of homes. Not much was discarded. It was usefully recycled before the term was even popularized.

Dedicated in 1916, this fine brick building was the new home to St. Michael School, serving students through eighth grade. Far from the modest cost of $75, records indicate this building cost around $34,000. The school grounds included restrooms for boys on one side of the building and girls on the other. The small facilities are visible in the picture.

Some of the students attending St. Michael's posed for this picture on the steps with a nun who was likely their instructor. The girls are sporting their Mary Janes and saddle shoes while some of the boys are wearing neckties. At the time, overalls and blue jeans were not worn as fashion statements and would likely have been unacceptable school attire. They all appear to be wearing a smile.

St. Michael's had a children's choir. They took this picture in 1927 on what must have been a cool day since they are all seen wearing light coats and fashionable hats. Singers with family names such as Seberger, Doctor, Peifer, Kaiser, Mager, Bohney, Hilbrich, Schweitzer, Grimmer, Govert, and Thiel were among the young ladies posed with Sister Adolphina.

Something that was new at one time eventually becomes something old. Not all structures can be salvaged, restored, or repurposed. The St. John Township School No. 2 has moved around and remains useful as living history. St. Michael's School, however, met a different fate. The brick structure was replaced with a modern facility, and the old building was torn down in 1984. Although its physical presence ceased to exist once demolished and removed, decades of memories remain, many of them captured in pictures. The most cherished memories, however, are those that live on in the hearts and minds of the hundreds of students who walked its halls.

St. John Township area teenage students attended Dyer Central High School. In 1915, this class picture was taken of five young ladies, some of whom were likely from Schererville. The high school served what became known as the Tri-Town area of St. John, Schererville, and Dyer. It was a forerunner to Lake Central High School, located in St. John and serving students within those same boundaries.

In this 1917 glimpse of Dyer Central High School, a long sidewalk approaches the main doors in front. The old building was located where Kahler Middle School sits today, one of three middle schools that make up part of the Lake Central system. The location is within the neighboring town of Dyer.

Vivian Voreacos was the Dyer Central librarian and an educator. When the high school organized a chapter of the Future Teachers of America (FTA) in the late 1950s, it appropriately named the chapter in her honor. Much like Voreacos, the local FTA chapter was designed to stimulate student interest in the teaching profession and to help its members understand the philosophy and ideals of educators.

The large complex in the background is Dyer Central, serving Tri-Town students. These young men photographed in 1948 were "the Dyer Eleven" football team. The size of the group was in direct contrast to the Lake Central High School (LCHS) teams of more recent seasons. By the 1990s, there were many occasions when other high schools came to LCHS and were intimidated by the sheer number of athletes comprising the team and bench.

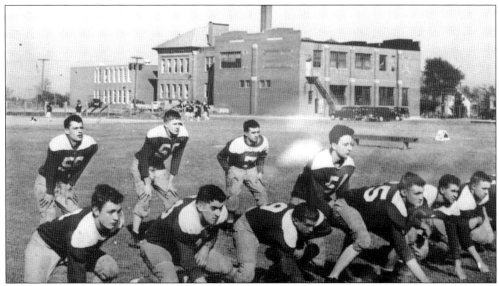

As the town continued to grow, so did membership in local places of worship. These young Communicants were posed in front of St. Michael the Archangel Catholic Church, the first church in town built by many of the original settlers. Local houses of worship not only create an environment of love and understanding within their walls, but also strive to be a viable component of the community.

Faith-based communities often sponsored humanitarian drives or civic-minded efforts for the greater good. Pictured here is a group of volunteers, mothers, and grandmothers. Many had family stationed overseas during World War II. They would get together under the spiritual guidance of Father Biegel to prepare packages for men and women at war. Many other groups such as the Greek Philoptochos Societies and Circles of Serbian Sisters did similar work.

In 1970, the St. George Serbian community bought vacant property at South Broad and Joliet Streets in the then unincorporated area of New Elliott. The land eventually became part of Schererville. Parishioners frequently gathered on the vacant property for picnics and other activities to enjoy the comradery and raise funds for a future church. Young people would often set up a softball game between chores such as clearing land.

Parishioners of St. George Serbian Orthodox Church on Joliet Street gathered in May 2011 to commemorate their church's patron saint. From their initial purchase of vacant land, they acquired additional acreage and built a hall, a social center, two homes, and this church. So many church members from Indiana Harbor settled in Schererville that a local developer named the adjacent subdivision Novo Selo, meaning "new village" in Serbian.

When St. Michael's was the only church in town, it was a nucleus of activity and, in many ways, still is today. As trustees of the church, the men in this 1927 photograph were also in a position of trust and leadership with the town. They are, from left to right, (seated) Nick Schafer; (standing) Peter Schweitzer, Bartel Schiessler, and Pete Kuhn.

Next to St. Michael's Church is the final resting place for many of its parishioners. The cemetery is a beautiful and tranquil site. It also offers a place for the living to escape the noises and distractions of life while respectfully visiting those at rest. Schererville's founding father, Nicholas Scherer, is one of them. He died in 1907 at the age of 76, and his wife, Frances, followed in 1911 at age 77.

Six

GROWTH

It is not very likely that the boundaries of Schererville will change again. But a lack of expansion does not mean a lack of progress. Since 1866, town borders have moved continually, sweeping outward over unincorporated areas surrounding the original settlement. Vacant land, farms, and homes were welcomed into the fold as becoming part of the town of Schererville was increasingly advantageous. Like a mother hen with her chicks, the town spread its wings and embraced its surroundings, offering security and services.

Now that borders are relatively fixed, the town is able to turn within to concentrate on improvements. Duties once performed by church trustees are now done by elected officials. Volunteers evolved into full-time firefighters serving from several fire stations. Police who once used a porch light for signals now employ a highly technical radio system, modern equipment, and a comparatively enormous staff. A town court has replaced the old justice of the peace system. The public works, wastewater, and parks and recreation departments effectively manage roadwork, water, refuse, recreation, and more.

This book is coming to an end, but every day is a new beginning for Schererville. With a nod of gratitude to those here in the 1800s, those once a part of town, those here now, and those yet to come, celebrating Schererville history, its periods of growth, and its present and future make the town of Schererville one of the best places to live in Lake County and the state of Indiana.

This old photograph is blurry and dark, but it cannot disguise the sunny future that the historic Lincoln Highway would mean for Schererville. Town resident John Thiel is shown leaning on a fancy car, pictured in front of the sign explaining why this portion of US 30 is known as the "Ideal Section."

This much more modern picture taken in 1997 shows that the Ideal Section of Lincoln Highway remains an important distinction for the area. This improvement is a bridge crossing on the south side, which was installed by and dedicated to the memory of the Hermon Tapp family. While it is a difficult place to stop during high traffic hours, motorists are often seen taking pictures of this landmark.

One of the reasons the Ideal Section was so named was because it was designed as a modern model for solid road construction. It included drainage, lighting, sidewalks, and roadbed concrete at least eight inches thick, making it an ideal road for travel. When part of it was being torn up and replaced in the late 1990s, historian Art Schweitzer was on hand with a measuring tape.

When a portion of the Ideal Section was reopened in November 1996, Watson School students were on hand to witness the breaking of a champagne bottle and cutting of ribbons. Pictures were snapped, news media were present, and cheers filled the air. Over 25 years later, many of the youngsters still travel over this road regularly.

While roads like US 30 brought a lot of growth for the town, that same growth, in turn, created a need for more roads. Some of the proposed new roads were in direct response to the population explosion and others were needed to alleviate ever-increasing traffic issues on main routes. It was decided to extend Seventh-Seven Avenue from US 41 on the east to St. John Road/Patterson on the west. The project turned out to be a major challenge because of the swampy land between the north-south routes that had to be crossed. Engineers specializing in such an undertaking were brought in and construction got underway. Although the "floating" road presented problems, the project was finally completed thanks to a layer cake of items, including a poly material, that comprise the roadbed.

In 1994, the iron bridge was already seen by many as a landmark. It stood there for 60 years. Coming south from Highland on US 41, it was the last overpass before reaching US 30. Heading north takes the driver out of Schererville into Highland. It was considered a smart route north and south, as drivers could avoid waiting for trains.

As this picture demonstrates, US 41 was a main artery, heavily traversed day and night. On the right ahead of the heavy equipment, the earth was being moved to accommodate the iron bridge replacement. Traffic was not disrupted as much as one might expect while the new bridge was in construction.

According to reports, nearly 2,000 people were on hand to witness the demolition of the old familiar iron bridge. Early on the morning of June 21, 2001, puffs of smoke blasted out of the key spots, causing the old structure to sink down on itself without endangering the new construction to its east or the witnesses to the west.

Coordinating the entire process with the railroad officials, several layers of engineers, construction teams, and government leadership, the old iron bridge came to rest. It settled down on the very ground it had passed over for about 67 years. The final demolition crew had a scant 16 hours to disassemble and remove the remains in order to clear the tracks for regular train traffic.

This aerial view taken around 2001 shows how change is constant. This is US 30 east of US 41. The road crisscrossing like a snake is Joliet Street, the historic Lincoln Highway. When US 30 was modernized, it was relocated and straightened out in numerous places. In the foreground is the Bank of Highland, which later became Sand Ridge Bank and then First Financial. Like the town, things keep changing. Beyond the railroad overpass, Walgreens is visible. However, the restaurant building between there and the tracks was not yet built. The underpass, designed for drivers to avoid train traffic, was a problem point during heavy rains as the dip in the highway would fill with water slow to recede. Drivers often made the mistake of thinking they could manage it and would need to be rescued. Near the upper right-hand side of the picture, Teibel's restaurant and the Crossings of Schererville are on either side of US 41. The outbuildings on the southwest corner of the intersection were not yet constructed.

There was another railroad underpass on Seventy-Third Avenue or Old Lincoln Highway near Burr Street on the east side of town. It frequently flooded, just like the underpass on US 30 after heavy rains. In this 1984 photograph, a school bus en route to Andrean High School simply did not make it. The students on board were able to exit the bus and swim to higher ground.

These are the Andrean High School students who managed to escape the water-logged school bus and get to safety. A diver was brought in to search for a "missing" student who turned out to be already standing on dry ground. Today, the train tracks and underpass are but a memory. The roadbed was leveled and the train tracks removed, making way for a bike and walking path.

Between Wilhelm and Joliet Streets, a marker is seen on a wall built by the Works Progress Administration. The WPA often marked its contribution by signing it and engraving the year of completion. Once a sign of progress, some of the WPA's projects have been demolished over the decades to make room for modern-day replacements. Others still stand strong.

The New York Central double tracks crossing town could have been a blockade to the children who would walk from their homes on the west side to attend school, located on the east side. Fortunately, this short-cut tunnel affectionately described as "the Hole in the Wall," provided a quick route. According to *Schererville Through the Years*, it was often a little daunting given the imaginations of children.

Markers of different sorts are all around Schererville, one just needs to know where to find them and what they mean. Some of them are a part of history, and others are still in use today. Just like highways with mile markers along their routes, the railroads also need signs to pinpoint exact locations. Above, Dave Andrews (left) and Art Schweitzer (right) pose at mile marker 280, which stood there longer than the tracks. Below, at marker 281 of the Pennsylvania Railroad, Steve Orban (left) is pictured with Dave Andrews (right). The location is marked in stone and, with larger numerals, easier to see from a passing train.

Railroads were as much the lifeblood of communities as roads and trails. They brought goods from one area to another throughout the entire country. They transported people long before automobiles became a common mode of transportation. But as the automobile industry grew and influenced the way people lived and moved around, many of the railroad tracks fell into disrepair as certain routes were unused. It is easy to see the difference in these two pictures between a well-used track and one that became stagnant. In many towns, trolley tracks were paved over as the attractive and useful trolleys were retired in favor of diesel-guzzling buses.

Remnants of a once useful railroad track are nearly completely overtaken by nature in this picture taken in 1996. The abandoned tracks used to cross land owned by Nicholas Scherer. The line was used to deliver supplies and heavy equipment right to downtown Schererville. Eventually, all traces of the tracks were removed when the new police station was completed and the parking lot paved.

Popularized as "Rails to Trails," much of America saw old railroad beds transformed into bike paths and walking trails. The Pennsy Greenway trail crosses over several miles within Schererville in a re-imagination of the space. The route includes benches, a rest area, and scenic views and can take the enthusiast through Redar Park, downtown Schererville, and Rohrman Park. The final phase kicked off in 2022.

Picnics, parades, and huge gatherings have always been part of the fabric that weaves Schererville into one lovely community. In this early-20th-century picture, one can clearly see St. Michael's School in the background. Style of dress and types of cars help estimate dates, making it possible this picnic took place in the 1920s.

Although this photograph might trick one into thinking it was taken much earlier, the pavement tells the truth. This was part of a bicentennial parade celebrating 200 years of the United States of America in 1976. The scene is a depiction of what the country's early settlers looked like when they passed through Schererville.

This classic photograph shows early Schererville residents Bernard and Sophia Schulte standing in front of their meat market at Joliet and Mary Streets. The younger man on the left is their son Bernard II, who also ran the shop. When the building was torn down, the lumber was saved and reused for a home for Bernard III. The family remained at the same location, firmly planted in the town. Vernon and Wilma Schulte actively volunteered with the Schererville Historical Society.

Peter Cope was the second officially appointed marshal in Schererville, following Michael Steuer, who served the community for two years from 1925 to 1927. According to the history of the town's police department, his uniform "was said to be a black vest and a star." He used his personal Model T Ford to cruise around town. Cope lived on Wilhelm Street near the center of everything. At the time of this writing, the chief of police is Peter Sormaz.

While most malls and shopping centers have an anchor store, Gard's was an anchor for downtown Schererville. The business was started in 1879. By 1918, the building was enlarged and moved more than once to its current location on Junction Avenue across from town hall. A very enterprising man, George Gard also ran a coal business, using his truck for deliveries.

Not far from Gard's was this classic place once known as Louie Meyer's Tavern and Dance Hall. It was used for parties, receptions, and weekly dances. The Schererville Historical Society honored the building with a postcard that says, "From the '30s and into the '50s it was the place to be on a Saturday night." The location was 40 East Joliet Street. It has been beautifully renovated.

These men stand at the service station that once was at the southeast corner of Joliet Street and Cline Avenue when Joliet Street was the Lincoln Highway. It was a full-service station selling Texaco gasoline. This station was owned and operated by Matt Seberger. Once US 30 was relocated farther south, business was not as brisk, and the station eventually closed.

When Joliet Street was still part of the Lincoln Highway, gas stations were plentiful and all of them did well. Immediately across the street from the Smiling Service Station, Mathias and Marie Seberber put up this building on the northeast corner of Joliet Street and Cline Avenue. The building, which had living quarters in the basement, is still in use today as a convenience store.

This Shell Gas Station was in operation in 1949, located less than a mile south of the Old Lincoln Highway on the new route of modern US 30. It was operated by owner Joseph Reiplinger. Later, the site was home to Rollin' On RV Sales and Service, billed as the largest recreational vehicle business in the state. Today, RVs are still sold there under the business name Pete's RV Center.

In this earlier photograph at the corner of Cline Avenue and US 30 sits a large lumber business known as Schererville Lumber & Supply Company. It was similar to its sister company Highland Lumber & Supply. It remained in operation for over 40 years. Then, in 1995, Von Tobel Lumber & Hardware took over the site and did some remodeling; it is open for business today.

Ace Hardware was once one of the only places in town for hardware. It was located on the west side of US 41 south of US 30. Over time, big-box stores moved into town, giving customers the options of Home Depot, Lowe's, Menard's, and others. Ace closed, reopened for a while as a Corvette sales store, and is now BBCE, a hugely successful baseball card exchange business.

In 1961, discount stores were a new concept. When Mays opened at the northwest corner of US 30 and US 41, it was a major event. Big Top Super Foods was also in this shopping center. Eventually, Strack and Van Til Supermarket and Walgreens Pharmacy took over the space. When they vacated, nothing sat empty for long. The location attracts tenants, and the center remains fully occupied today.

Sometimes change is so subtle that one does not notice it much at the time. From the very beginning, downtown Schererville has undergone a tremendous amount of change, yet the town somehow keeps its original charm. Stores and their owners come and go, what they sell changes, storefronts get new faces, buildings put on additions, taverns and restaurants modernize, and old windows are covered with new awnings. The main street, once dusty and slightly crooked, has been dug out, elevated, and replaced. Wide sidewalks have replaced hitching posts. Some buildings have been razed, and others have been completely relocated. The mixture of original structures, modern improvements, and latest additions all together are still recognizable as historic downtown Schererville.

Someone must have taken great pride in the finishing of the roadbed on Joliet Street in 1911. They would have no way of knowing it would later be covered over with concrete. In 1999, Ray Berilla held up a piece of the original road during the work of another improvement project on Joliet Street in downtown Schererville.

A few years after Joliet Street was improved, another project was underway—not in the street, but alongside it. In 2002, workers were photographed laying the blocks and bricks that would become the clock tower in front of the new town hall. The old Gard's store was already turned to face Junction Avenue but has since changed its face, too.

It is commonplace to see cranes in big cities, and they are always associated with signs of progress and growth. This crane was lifting what was likely an air-conditioning unit onto the roof of a new building. Like an eagle's nest up high, one can see the American flag flapping proudly during construction.

When the new town hall was at last finished in 2003, downtown Schererville had a modern refinement. The clock tower and the flagpoles stand tall near the corner, gracing it with charm. The columns at the front doors give the brick building its official government flare, but the architecture also welcomes visitors inside like an old friend on the original dusty road.

In 1909, when this picture was taken, Schererville's downtown looked exactly like what it was, a farming community. Downtown was central for the residents of the time, but it was surrounded by open fields and sand dunes that would transform into what is seen today. Homes, businesses, paved roads, and people would find their way to Schererville over the decades to come.

This open field was once somebody's backyard. Today, it is a fairway on Scherwood Golf Course. Not every inch of open ground was completely covered by buildings and pavement. The golf course and many beautiful parks throughout town are some of what remains of the fields that were once farmed by original settlers.

Schererville's parks and recreation department hosts the historic Hilbrich Log Cabin on its site. The cabin was relocated near the parks' offices, which are inside the community center. It was preserved using almost all its original material. The cabin is available for visitation and planned programs. People can learn about Schererville's past by visiting the cabin and walking in the footsteps of early town settlers.

Today, the parks and recreation department is responsible for numerous parks throughout town. It manages more than 260 acres of land in 28 parks. The department has grown in perfect sync with the town. Sports facilities, recreation equipment and programs, paved trails, and picnic shelters are just part of what it offers. The department preserves the past through the cabin and provides the best in the present as it continually plans ahead.

The more recent past is also remembered in town. In this picture, Richard Krame points out the commemorative plaque installed for the celebration at the crossroads during America's bicentennial in 1976. Krame served the town for decades in many capacities, including on the town council, as a police commissioner, and as town manager. His civic interests and service have helped the town expand and blossom.

Schererville not only honors and remembers its own, but joins efforts throughout the state, county, and country. These firemen paid homage to those first responders and others who lost their lives in the September 11, 2001, attack on America in New York. People gathered again on the 20th anniversary to offer prayers in a solemn ceremony at the 9-11 memorial in town.

These graceful deer crossing Janice Drive near US 30 are clinging to some of the only vacant wooded property remaining in their habitat. They struggle for space as humankind encroaches on the once wild land. To help solve that and similar issues, the town has donated hundreds of thousands dollars to help develop Lake Hills County Park. The plan includes a native prairie and restored savanna, indicating Schererville's development will have come full circle. (Photograph by Ray Radoja.)

There are not enough pages in this book to include all that is great about the town of Schererville. There is a welcome sign at nearly every major road leading into Schererville, and their messages are meant sincerely. Visit and learn more about the town. Become part of Schererville's history by being here. Welcome to Schererville.

DISCOVER THOUSANDS OF LOCAL HISTORY BOOKS FEATURING MILLIONS OF VINTAGE IMAGES

Arcadia Publishing, the leading local history publisher in the United States, is committed to making history accessible and meaningful through publishing books that celebrate and preserve the heritage of America's people and places.

Find more books like this at
www.arcadiapublishing.com

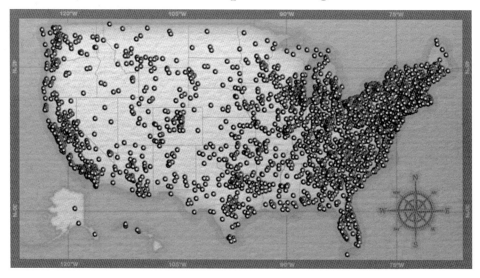

Search for your hometown history, your old stomping grounds, and even your favorite sports team.